Mar 23 2016

Credit Suisse announced that it plans to fire 6000 of its employees. Year To Date 2800 terminated.

Mar 30 2016

A steel major announced exit from Britain. 15,000 jobs on the line...

40,000 more jobs affected.

Cameron calls emergency cabinet meet.

The downward spiral. It has started...

PIAM CREATIONS

THE COMING STORM

GLOBAL STOCK MARKET CRASH: 2016-2018.

A BRIEF.

A precursor in the beginning of 2016. From the middle 2016 — late 2016 the crisis will be out in the open, early 2017 the situation worsens, only to hit the lowest point in mid - late 2017. We will be a mute witness to the spectacle of an economic holocaust of our generation.

Cause and effect. Indicators and outcome. This is the an economic diagnosis done on the basis of an objective analysis of the symptoms. I have diagnosed and have outlined the process on how I have reached the conclusion. Everything is open in front of you and as you turn page after page you can see your collective economic destinies unfold before your eyes.

Wear your logic and analyze. Everyone can reach a conclusion. I have reached a conclusion. You read and decide.

BECAUSE ONLY IF YOU KNOW YOU CAN ACT.

<u>Early Warning : Stay Alert. Early Warning : Stay Alert.</u>

One thing will shock you – the speed. Fast and furious. It gives you no second chance.

From now on economy as life will have to be managed with an eye on cause and effect. Whatever we do will comeback to us with a multiplier.

Early Warning Stay Alert.

The Global Economic Crisis Simplified. So You Know What To Do.

What Can You Do Now ? To Minimize The Damage .

THE COMING CRASH.

Let's begin with China. Because this is where it all began. Till one fine day in the last quarter of 2017 it will reach the nadir. The lowest point.

On February 12 2016 as I write this, the world witnessed just the beginning of the great fall that will culminate in the worst unimaginable economic disaster of this millennium.

On February 11 2016 Janet Yellen chaired a meet of the US Federal Reserve. During the meet, news channels were abuzz - 'China faced its worst year of economic growth in a quarter century. Oil went down again putting a question mark on the oil centric economies of Russia, Brazil and the Middle East. Wall Street closed to the worst ever start to a year.'

Gold spiked.

This is what has happened. I will now tell you what will happen and how you can mitigate the effect and take precautions so that you don't end up on the wrong side of the biggest economic disaster in your lifetime. I would rather people debate the process and the indicators rather than result.

There will be 3 big dates. In the mid 2016-last quarter of 2016 we will enter the last lap of a familiar terrain. The first dip to herald the start of the Big Fall. From then on we will be holding on to straws to escape the cyclonic winds of an economic downturn. In the beginning of 2017 the second fall will confirm our worst fears. In the last quarter of 2017 the 3rd fall will enter 2017 in history books as the year when the global economic recession happened.

Exactly a century back we had the World War 1. The cataclysmic event a century later is not a nuclear war as has been the fear but an economic depression.

An economic holocaust ?

The Gold Surge.

On 11 Feb 2016 the stocks fell and gold spiked. Imagine the spike when the markets fall is 5 times more. The spike will be proportionate and more.

Feb 2016

News: Stocks are down in the dumps the world over, bonds are rallying and the yen is shining. It was a catastrophic night for the financial districts. And going by the early signs, it won't be a pretty morning as markets are sliding again...

News: Worldwide stocks stumbled on fears over the health of the global economy. The global equity benchmark index closed more than 20 per cent below its record high in 2015.

News: It is confirmed global stocks are in a bear market.

An all-country world equity index, which tracked shares in 45 nations hit its lowest level in more than two and a half years.

Nature has given us many years and more opportunities to take effective action. But when we don't, it steps in and makes sure we pay for the economic sins we have committed.

In 2116 economists may well point back and laugh at the fools who managed the global economy in the first two decades of this century; those who imagined they could trick people and nature. Or did they really believe that their action was the answer to combat the 2008 recession.

Time and again history has proved to us to this adage 'Every rise has a fall.'

I would like to clarify: Every 'false' rise has a fall.

It was but to be expected.

Let me explain.

The rise is false. It is a bubble.

Just as a rise is indicative of yet another rise, the dip is an indicator of another.

China, USA, Europe, Japan and Middle East. Let's journey.

China Implodes.

Problems arising from China have metastasized globally crashing stock and commodity markets and disrupting high yield sectors.

The iron ore that China gulped from Rio de Janeiro to Australia was misutilised to build mega fetal cities. Fetal - unborn. The 'unborn cities' that became infamous across the globe as the 'ghost cities of China'. The world's second biggest economy built cities after cities, cities after cities, hundreds of them but not a single person chose to stay. Unborn, unused and unusable. Homes, restaurants, malls, gladiatorial stadia that should have been bustling with vibrant people were mute witness to empty space.

It took some time before the world became aware of the fetal cities of China. It seemed more fictional than truth.

China's infrastructure driven growth of two decades costed billions and led to a cascading worldwide boom starting off with commodity prices.

Were the 'unborn cities' at the core of this global boom? A scary thought. Imagine the money that has gone in and no output. The debt cities of China.

The showpiece of an economic boom will surely add dead weight to the sinking ship of China and global economy.

The stupendous growth was in large measure due to debt funded projects that gave no returns. Debt was funded by bonds, many of which were collateralized with copper. And copper is down in the dumps. So neither is there a ROI nor is there value in the collateral. Debt recovery is a distant dream.

More the debt more the trouble. We all want to hide our debts. But sooner or later it will come out in the open. Then all mayhem breaks loose. Like it did.

The Chinese economy posted growth of 6.9% in 2015, its slowest rate since 1990. The economic slowdown has led investors to move their money out to get better returns. China's forex reserves are down by a whopping 700 billion dollars.

The December manufacturing PMI revealed a sluggish industrial production for the 10th consecutive month. This led to the 2016 downslide of the Chinese equity markets and along with it the global equity markets.

Marc Faber, the author of 'Gloom and Doom Report' says that 'the Chinese economy was heading for a hardlanding, as borrowers piled up debt and were finding it difficult to pay interest.'

George Soros stated that the current Chinese situation "amounts to a crisis" and brings memories of the recession of 2008. "China is struggling to find a new growth model and its currency devaluation is transferring problems to the rest of the world." Soros has blamed the Chinese economy for global bearishness.

Commodity expert Jim Rogers: "The US stock market was down last year. This started in the US and Europe. China is just catching up in a big-big way."

China is releasing huge cash into its financial system due to a continuing financial turmoil in an effort to stem the tide. But you cannot treat a cancer with intravenous fluids.

The Chinese fear a quick devaluation of their currency. It could destabilise their economy. Chinese central bank governor Zhou Xiaochuan has accused "speculative forces" of targeting the yuan.

The last time China devalued Renminbi, it caused the Asian currency crisis.

China challenges a currency trader. Not to bet against the Renminbi.

George Soros may be legendary.

Yet you are left with a niggling thought: The mighty colossus challenges a mere trader! Why should a colossus even acknowledge let alone take cognizance of a trader of currencies.

Because it is afraid. Yes. China is scared!

China is scared because it is unfolding and doesn't know what to do.

'China is in the midst of a triple bubble, with the third-largest credit bubble of all time, the largest investment bubble and the second-largest real-estate bubble.' This is a Credit Suisse analysis.

George Soros is a legendary investor.

In 1992, he became known as the man who "broke" the Bank of England. He gained $1 billion betting that the pound would collapse.

What do you think George Soros has done in 2016.

He has shorted the Renminbi in a big way.

Ding Dong.

China is unfolding. Stay Alert.

USA Uncertain.

February 11 2016. Janet Yellen chaired a meet in which it was observed that if the recent dire global economic indicators continued it could be multiplying downside risk to the USA.

The Bureau of Labor Statistics reported that the unemployment rate dropped to an eight-year low and that the number of new hires and voluntary quits in the U.S. recently climbed to a nine-year high.

There were three rounds of quantitative easing (QE). QE1 was from 2008 to 2010. The US Fed bought $2.1 trillion of treasury bonds and mortgage-backed securities. This stopped when the Fed indicated that there was improvement in the economy.

But the recovery proved to be false. So QE 2 was on. It started in November 2010 and lasted till the middle of 2011. During QE2 the US Fed bought $600 billion of bonds comprising mostly mortgage-backed securities.

After a little more than a year the Fed realized there was no real recovery.

So it started QE3 in late 2012 and during this program the Fed pumped in $85bn per month. The Fed began reducing those purchases at the start of 2015.

The Fed has spent more than $4trillion in buying bonds.

There is a broad consensus that QE1 was a success - it was quite big: a couple of trillion dollars, and lasted quite long: a couple of years. It helped in preventing the 2008 recession becoming worse than it was.

A research study found that QE2 was only a third as effective as QE1.

The San Francisco Federal Reserve Bank, found that QE2 added just 0.13 percentage points to the annual rate of economic growth in 2010, which was at 2.8% when the program was implemented.

The Fed had prolonged QE3. And it may prove to be the unwanted QE. The QE that did the damage. The QE that broke the back of the camel and stopped the caravan.

Money at low rates leads to speculation. It would be a fallacy to think that highs of the US stock markets are not in large measure due to the QE.

Now that the QE is not there where do you imagine the US stocks are headed?

Just stand back and take a deep breath.

There is not much time left to get out of the stock market.

Andrew, a former manager of the Fed's mortgage-buying scheme, has commented that low rates may not helped ordinary Americans.

Was Wall Street was sucking in most of the extra cash.

Greed. A cardinal sin. In modern times greed has been one of the cardinal sins that has been most accepted among the educated class. But then a cardinal sin never goes without leaving a trail. The time is near. The time has arrived.

Printing money in the world's biggest economy also had an impact on global economies.

In a study of 65 countries European Central Bank, found that QE1 and QE2 led to spillovers in advanced economies across the globe.

The study revealed found that while QE1 led investors to invest into the US while QE2 led investment into emerging economies. Now that the source of easy money is shut scores of countries are feeling the easy money withdrawal syndrome. The tap is dry and they are feeling blanked out.

The men at the helm want a pat on the back all the while and there was no one to bold enough to bite the bullet. Not that they did not know.

They just didn't have the guts to bite the bullet.

A lot of Americans want Donald Trump as president. Would he have this support if the situation had been different. Yes, terrorism apart has not the economic mismanagement led people to look towards a businessman to spruce up the system in Washington.

Hillary Clinton may be the bettor's choice but Trump is a creation of his times. And creation of the times however eccentric have been known to be unusually powerful.

We all can read faces. I have seen only Trump's photograph.

'The future president?!!" Umm. I am left confused. Uneasy. Something unusual. Somewhat pragmatic. Promising. Very correct. Very incorrect. Swings of a pendulum. Extremes. Some Unpredictable. Maybe…

Decipher that. Put him on the global scale.

Hillary has a chesire cat grin, nowadays The thought pokes her to smile. 'Lack of serious competition.' But then a sizeable population has also voted her opponents. She cannot be laid back.

She needs to back her intent with action. And she needs to erase 'More of the same?' tag that comes with her.

Ben Bernanke spent $3 trillion to make the NYSE a bull market for half a dozen years. Janet Yellen hiked the interest rate by a quarter point and the bull market tanked by a third of its value.

So weak is the stock market.

"The world is an uncertain place, and all monetary policymakers can really be sure of is that what will happen is often different from what we currently expect.": Stanley Fischer, the No. 2 at the U.S. Federal Reserve.

USA Uncertain...

Europe Lives In Delusion.

Feb 2016

News: 'SocGen leads European banks lower at the close as rout resumes on Deutsche, Barclays, HSBC, Lloyds and RBS share prices.'

Europe's top banks are down in the dumps. And that is putting the case lightly. Deutsche Bank's share went down lower than its recession price and the convertible bonds are way down. Standard Chartered's share price is at its lowest in nearly 20 years.

The Swiss bank Credit Suisse stock was down 43 percent over the last year and touched a 27-year low. If Credit Suisse tries to sell their bonds they will get junk rates. Their trading income is abysmal.

In UK, HSBC, Lloyds, Barclays and RBS tell a similar story.

Falling off a cliff. Since the beginning of 2016, the Stoxx Europe 600 Banks Index, has lost 27 per cent.

If you had invested in banks a decade ago you would have not made a profit.

After 2008 the economy in developed countries was not exciting. So banks turned to emerging Asian and African economies providing them eight years of easy money. But borrowers are struggling,

Now, increasingly borrowers in millions don't have the money to repay.

The problem with banks is − they ask you to take a loan and then they want you to pay it back whether you have the money or not.

Was there any forecast. Any sort of analysis? Could the banks not even foresee the effect of providing money at a flow? Banks have created a bubble that will burst in their face in May 2016.

Watch the global equity markets in the middle of the year. Watch Deutsche in May 2016.

The credit default swap (CDS) of Deutsche has risen to high levels. This means that the cost of insuring against a default by Deutsche has risen considerably.

Flashback 2008: Remember the banks which fell. Some of them never got up. Be careful which bank you put your money.

The moon is a safe place. There are no banks on the moon.

They will drive you mad the banks. Banks will go down and they will take with them everything else.

Just get out of them.

Why does common sense get the kick when it comes to managing global economy?

The European Central Bank (ECB) increases its very own quantitative easing, piling on public debt to the private debt it has already accumulated. The ECB has planned to increase its QE from $14 billion to €60 billion until at least September of 2016.

It has failed in US. It has failed in Japan. Still the ECB is at it. This will only create a spiral of problems. It will act as a multiplier of dangerous economic perils.

Clever people learn from others mistakes, fools from their own and idiots never.

The more you blow a bubble the bigger it gets. The bigger a bubble balloon the louder it will burst.

ECB is blowing the cash bubble. More and more. Harder and harder. The bigger it gets the worse will be the explosion. Madness. Bouts of delusions.

Europe lives in delusion...

The Gulf Deficit

Oil. It seems fantasy that oil costed more than 100 dollars just a couple of years back. When it touched 40 the venerable sheiks wished that was the bottom. Now it has breached and take my word it will get below 10.

They survive on oil. And oil will never bounce back. Never.

Notwithstanding what the reputed consultants say. They say there is a chance of oil coming back.

I state here oil will never go back. The era of oil is over. Done.

Humanity has to look ahead, look elsewhere. One day or the other, oil had to be exhausted. We discovered engines and invented modern ways to use oil just a 100 - 150 years ago. In the span of human history this is like a blip click. Life is fragile. Life is transient.

In 2015 its budget deficit nearly reached $ 100 billion. Now, Saudi Arabia is looking for a $6 billion and $8 billion loan.

In 2016 six of the rich Arab economies could borrow upto $20 billion. Till now they were the lenders to the world. This is the state of affairs when oil touched 40. Imagine when oil falls below 30 dollars and then below 20 dollars and then below 10 dollars.

And these have nil else to prop their economy. The venerable sheiks put all their eggs in the oil basket. The future looks bleak for them.

Oil is an exhaustible energy source. Alternative energies are the future of civilization. Governments the world over are promoting alternative energies. Technology is gaining fast. If we get to air travel on alternative energy that will be the end of oil as the major source of transport energy that connects existence East to West and North to South.

Countries have to reduce carbon imprints. Clean energy.

Humans are done with oil. It is written in the sky. The era of oil is over.

One era to another.

The gulf widens...

Asia In Doldrums

Feb 2016

News: Has Japan's grand attempt to reflate the world's third largest economy failed? The Bank of Japan (BOJ) crossed over into uncharted territory, pushing interest rates below zero for the first time ever.

For the first time ever.

In just two days the Japanese stock market was down nearly 8%. The GDP figures indicated that the Japanese economy was shrinking again.

There is a strange problem in Japan where large corporations are sitting of piles of cash - as much as 3 trillion. But are not spending it. Because they are afraid their investment will not get returns in the current and the foreseeable future. The corporates in Japan know the economy is on a downswing.

Hold on to dear money !

15 Feb 2016

This Indian bank posted a quarterly net loss of Rs 3,342 crore, the largest loss in the Indian banking history. This was indicative of the entire set of public sector banks in India.

Exports in Asian giants Japan, China and South Korea drop by double digits.

We all know the China story.

Asia in doldrums...

The Global Rout

Places to hide. To escape the avalanche of the economic holocaust.

Corporates need to forecast downward graphs. We can't keep going up all the time. The economy moves in cycles. Study of the cyclical trends of modern economic history should be the baseline for every management executive. The reasons for the ebb and flow of modern economy has to be analyzed and the rise and fall has to be factored in.

Some executives are known to take hundreds of millions of dollars in bonuses. Executives live the high life and we know some buy islands for them to frolick around. I have nil against that provided it is all well earned (and not by insider trading). And shared.

If you don't share you go down. One more time nature will teach us this lesson in 2016-2018.

Yet again. Yet one more time.

Spread the wealth. To the have nots. The cosmos means business. And we all better listen. And imbibe.

The Armageddon

Cornerstone Macro technical analyst Carter Worth told CNBC's "Fast Money" traders. "When you see the relative performance of utilities, bonds and the S&P 500 index acting opposite to each other, you're about to get another contraction,"

The correlation between these three factors as well as gold and corporate bonds was analyzed. Carter stated that each divergence and contraction took place during periods of recession.

Not only has he predicted a deep recession but goes on to say: "It's very hard to reverse it."

It is destiny. Economic destiny is a pet theme of this book.

'The results of every action are etched at the time of the action itself.'

The world's best are trying all they can and more. Every trick and every tactic. And find that it all spills up in their faces.

Economics is destiny.

Destiny puts you in your place. If you have done right you will be in the right place. If you have done wrong you will be in the wrong place.

Skill yourself. Make yourself useful at whatever level you are in. Do right to yourself. Then do right to your community. Then you might find yourself in the right place when you meet destiny face to face.

Global economics is global destiny.

Central banks are running 'out of ammunition'.

CNN Money 9 Feb 2016

'They're pumping money into their economies, creating negative interest rates and buying billions of dollars in bonds. Yet experts are worried these strategies will not be enough to turn around the slump in the world.'

"As soon as the markets realize that the Fed and the ECB are out of ammunition, it's over," Stockman said. "I think we're in an extremely unsafe world — we've never been here before."

This is by a former US government Director of Budget.

'We are getting into a place where we have never been before.'

The Armageddon.

Voodoo Economics

They are manufacturing cash out of thin air. The voodoo economists.

It failed in Japan and it failed in USA. Yet the ECB is gung ho about it.

QE1 was useful. We should have bitten the bullet then. QE2 and QE3 were largely pumping money that was used to create a sense of well being. Like being on steroids.

The more the delay the more the spread of the cancer. The cancer has spread to all over. The different surgeons know this. But no one is ready to do the surgery. Because the patient may die on the operating table. So they continue to make the patient feel that all is well. Until he is alive.

We the common people are the patient. You and I. The common folks. The surgeons know it. That is the economists and the guys in the central banks. They know the cancer has spread all over the global economy.

And we are staring at best a recession, a depression and at worst a holocaust. They don't want to operate, they don't want to take a decision because the patient may die on the operating table.

The worry that the flood of cash has encouraged needless risky financial decisions is real. And the result of this easy money on emerging economies is an illusion.

Illusion of cash. Illusion of investment. Illusion of economy.

We have created an illusionary global economy. The cosmos is uncomfortable with illusions. Its basic nature is to get back to reality. Sooner or later.

Watch out for 2016 − 2018. The cosmos attempts to get back to reality with a crash.

2016 − 2018 : The Coming Crash.

The Kindergarten Class

Lets us go back down memory lane for a while and remember what they taught us at kindergarten: Reap what you sow.

When corporates made super profits did they give it back to their sharcholders in equal measure? Did they give it back to their stakeholder and the community in equal measure.

Actually it is economic common sense and doesn't need an MBA to figure out that money spread over a population, goes around and keeps the engines of a community humming.

When banks offered you loans did they eye only their chart busting profits?

This is a problem in Africa when banks rushed in and gave loans. No matter what.

When big corporates showed signs of default were they categorized as such in the balance sheet or were they hidden under some accounting jargon. Which means when the banks showed profit they were actually in loss. Did they hide it?

Remember kindergarten: Do Not Lie.

When large corporates defaulted were the loans collected or the big fish let off or worse more loans were offered. This is a problem in Asia. Where big fish are let off.

Remember in kindergarten: Do the right action.

We have put on the viewing glass of a kindergarten kid.

Does it look silly? You bet. And now you say will not the people in 2116 look back and laugh at us.

Right now, I don't know whether to cry or laugh. Coz it might even be funny if the situation were not so serious.

The Result.

Zero interest rate regimes has led to over-production. The over supply has led to less prices and more consumption. A consumption not driven by need contributes to the formation of a bubble.

To escape the effects of the 2008 recession the United States took to QE. Pump in easy money. With no real demand. By not withdrawing QE and taking their medicine in 2012 — market imbalances today are now bigger and the consequences greater.

It is like this - Treat the cancer early. The therapy is painful but the complications will be less.

Now the market has chronic osteoporosis. Breaks easily. Calcium deficiency. Not an appealing conditions to have.

The culprits are the banks (though they are not the only ones). This is where they started giving cash to create the cash illusion.

Which is the safe place. Whoever has reined in their banks. Who is that whoever. No one here.

The results can be read in the preparation. What you will be is in exponential proportion to what you do now.

You can judge the action by the result.

Glance at the 2016 results. And try to imagine what horrendous decisions over the last decade has led to these results.

Venezuela: 720 % inflation

Greece: Debt Crisis

China debt to GDP: 260%

USA: QE Bubble

Japan: Negative interest rates

Saudis: Lenders turn borrowers

The breadth of bad economic news spans the globe. From one end to another. With only a few islands of relief. These will also get dragged into the connected quagmire.

The stark landscape of history is a pointer to this immutable law.

From Goliath who fell to Lehmann bros which vanished.

You have to pay for your actions.

A stitch in time saves nine. The time has passed. Will the nine survive 2017? But the stitch didn't happen in time....

Utility

Availability of cash created an economy which did not have real utility. People created coz they had money not coz they had use or need for it. So you had ghost cities. Which fuelled a ghost economy and people didn't know of it until it became a ghostly news story.

The last trick was QE. QE was useful initially. In large part the QE had outlived its utility. Did the central banks carry out an analysis of the utility of QE every six months or every year?

No. They just had a blind shot.

But from now on the Cosmos will put utility on center stage. Right up there.

The fetal cities of China. The 'city planners', the 'masters of economy' the false creations of the commodity boom, the exports boom in several countries. The unborn cities will ring in the death knell of the modern mismanaged economy.

Pride precedes a fall.

Hey hold on. We need not build cities that will not be populated. Violation of the crucial economic principle : Useful. And Used.

Do something useful that will be used.

A fitness program that promotes health.

A preacher who is sincere.

A banker who gives a loan which gives ROI.

A clinical research which results in a drug that cures.

A goldsmith who crafts a design which is aesthetic.

A builder who designs a city which is smart.

An economist whose policy alleviates poverty.

A leader who implements.

A movie that people enjoy to watch.

An assassination which is globally applauded.

All these have utility. They are useful. They can be used.

Do our world leaders and economist and bankers need to be taught this basic lesson of human economic behavior. In our frenzy a penchant has grown, a temptation to make the simple convoluted. Making life complicated we have tied ourselves in a complex web that we are unable to get out of.

The more the convoluted the more the genius.

I would say the more the simple the more the genius.

A genius simply implements the complex.

Things are effective when they are useful and are used.

The next two years will reveal that utility is linked to survival.

Charles Darwin said rightly - Survival of the fittest. Be fit strategically, tactically, Hone your craft. Be technologically skilled. If you don't have a skill, create one.

The cosmos backs someone who is skilled. That is the priority of the Cosmos.

Those who are useful will be used. And will be paid for the use. Even in recession people will go that place which has nutritious food, to watch that movie which is entertaining and go to that doctor who gives accurate diagnosis.

Compact: This will make a strong comeback. The age of global banking is over for now. Banks will have to withdraw to survive. And shed to become lean.

Compact and utility will go hand in hand.

Keywords

- Survival of the skilled.

- 1 person business

- Family business

- Compact

- Utility

- Utility in luxury

- Skill

- Use

- Upgrade

- New use.

The skilled will survive. The very skilled will prosper.

Practice agriculture. You will be assured of food, housing and health. The small farm house. Being with nature and working on the farm is as healthy as it can get. And food can be a business.

Mar 2016. One of Wall Street's most accurate forecasters JP Morgan's Kolanovic predicts that stocks markets are in trouble. His choice of investment is gold.

The CEO of Euro Pacific Capital says the U.S. economy is in the midst of a recession that could turn out to be even more horrible than the Great Recession of 2008.

He is confident of only this option: gold. The safe haven.

Why gold? Because there is nil else of value left stupid!

Go For Gold.

If you wish to stay reasonable by the end of 2017 then head to the few places in the world that are relatively untouched.

Escape to India. This country has rallied behind one of the few world leaders worth his salt. Who says what he means and means what he says. Backed by the governor of RBI. They are investing in roads, trains and low cost housing. People will stay in these homes and generate an economy around them.

That economy which circulates within reasonable limits spikes within reasonable limits.

Or maybe Canada. Or the few such countries.

As per the latest survey people who live in Denmark, Norway, Sweden and Switzerland are the happiest in the world. Don't worry. Be happy. Head to Holland.

One more option. Escape.

Escape to reasonable countries.

Immigrate.

Limpid Eyed Cosmos

I had a bit cosmos hugging me today. Looking at me with limpid eyes. I was carrying her. She will save me from the harsh world. My 2 year girl going onto 3. Just about making sense of the world. But not touched by it. Hug your own cosmos, support them; they will be your saviors. When you look at their expectant innocent eyes and face with a look of belongingness. We will need to belong to those who belong to us. Just in case you have forgotten in the hurry to reach your targets.

Our targets will reach as low as they can get to teach us that interwoven is our life and we need to reach out to every human we come across in as natural a manner that nature ordained human behavior to be.

It seems apt to end where it all began. Targets.

What is your target. 'Your'.

What is the target of humanity? 'Humanity'.

You achieve your targets.

And allow humanity to achieve its.

What is humanity's target. Money, business, profit at any cost ?

Humane. Be humane. All the time. At any meet. At any conference. Any decision. Every pitch. Every tactic. Every strategy.

Be humane. Be humane.

The End Result.

Generate profit at any cost ? "Ha Ha."

The Last Minute. The Last Thoughts.

It will begin with the banks. And extend everywhere.

We will have ample time to think about this as the events unfold before our seemingly unbelieving eyes.

Basic lessons to world leaders, economists and bankers.

The culprits are the banks. They give money. And expect it back.

The chairman of Kingfisher airlines managed to leave India inspite of the country's police and law enforcement agencies on the lookout for him. He is living on a multiacre acre resort home in the United Kingdom. While his employees are running in circles for salaries not paid over a year. And banks left with huge unpaid loans. He comes to the table only after a huge public outcry.

Did we talk about executives who own islands while there are millions who rent a shelter on a day basis. Today I have a roof over my head when I sleep. Lucky me !

Are we the destined witness of an Economic Holocaust?

It is nature's way of purging excess and dead sloth greed from its system. Nature and Cosmos don't like these.

The moon is a safe place. I will go there. Because there are no banks on the moon.

QE: When everything fails we fall back on magic. Close your eyes. Open now. Hey we have more money! The voodoo economics of the voodoo economists

The stats are staggering.

Be brave and bite the bullet. We should have. The last chance was missed.

We will witness an economic holocaust.

Be ready for fly by wire decisions.

The End Result is an extrapolation of the initial decision multiplied by a factor.

The End Result is Upon Us. Wait and Watch. Or Get Out. Fast.

This time the recession will teach us to be humane.

Basically it is about the basics. Basics are the foundation. Basics are the building blocks. Basics are all there is. Basic is the end point.

You get the basic right you get everything right.

You decide your destiny at the time you act.

When the indicators are so bad the result cannot have a happy end.

Indicators are precursors of results. We can't have bad indicators and a good result. We can't have increased troponins and wish that the heart is normal. Right now the global economic indicators are the worst in 3 decades. Expect to have the worst recession in the past 30-50 years.

Life is fragile. Life is transient. Take this moment. Coz that is all you have.

What more do you want? Than be happy. Head to the happy countries.

One step in the right direction gives the strength for two steps in the right direction. Two steps in the right direction gives the strength for 4 steps in the right diection. 4 steps... Just substitute the word right with wrong and see where you end up.

Did the banks think that people will borrow from them and make profits out of a tentative economy? And pay them back for the banks to enjoy super profits! How dreamy! Or delusional ?

Global economy is global destiny.

America and the world never had it so bad in recent times. Sit up. And pray.

Sometimes the best comes out of the worst. Hope. Hope that we are in that situation right now.

Utilize every moment. These will never come back.

What we have been doing is against humanity's target. And there lies the crux of the problem and the biggest lesson the Cosmos is trying to teach us though the coming crash.

The End Result. Be Humane. Nothing else matters.

THE LAST QUOTES.

"I would liken the Fed to a blindfolded arsonist. Armed, danegrous and lost," the former director of the Office of Management and Budget, Stockman. Stockman has been a lynchpin of the US government during its heydays.

"As soon as the markets realize that the Fed and the ECB are out of ammunition, it's over." Stockman.

"I think we're in an extremely unsafe world — we've never been here before." Stockman

"Whoever replaces Barack Obama is going to inherit a worse recession than the one that he inherited from Bush," Schiff.

"A lot of the problems in the investment bank have been that people have been trying to generate revenue at all costs." Thiam, CEO Credit Suisse.

Generate revenue at any cost. "Ha Ha."- Piam.

IN THE WOMB OF THE END LIES A NEW BEGINNING – PIAM.

THE TECH SHIFT

BY PIAM

IN MAY 2016 in KINDLE * CREATESPACE

www.gipv.net

THE ADVENTURES OF THE ORANCZ TRIANGLEZ

PIAM CREATIONS

ANIMATION FILM IN SEP 2016

www.ingramcontent.com/pod-product-compliance
Lightning Source LLC
Chambersburg PA
CBHW080634190526
45169CB00009B/3385